NAUVOO
EXPOSITOR

NAUVOO EXPOSITOR

–THE TRUTH, THE WHOLE TRUTH,
AND NOTHING BUT THE TRUTH–

NAUVOO, ILLINOIS, FRIDAY, JUNE 7, 1844

VOL. 1, NO. 1

EDINA PUBLISHER'S NOTE:

This is a reprinting of the newspaper published in Nauvoo, Illinois which led to Joseph Smith's arrest and, indirectly, his death. Only one edition of the newspaper was ever printed. Joseph Smith called the newspaper a "nuisance" and said that the publishers had "formed a conspiracy for the purpose of destroying [his] life" [History of the Church, vol. 6, p. 432]. Joseph ordered the printing press destroyed and the order was carried out on June 10th, 1844. Joseph was arrested on June 25th and was killed by a mob on June 27, 1844.

The following was edited and put into novel format for readability. There are stories, news articles, and ads that have nothing to do with Joseph Smith, but they have been left in for accuracy.

This 2023 edition published by Edina Publishers LLC

ISBN 979-8-9884543-4-2 (print format)
ISBN 979-8-9884543-3-5 (ebook)

Cover design by Adrianna Schow
Manufactured in the United States of America

www.edinapublishers.com

CONTENTS

THE 'NAUVOO EXPOSITOR'...1

POETRY...2

    The Last Man.. 2

MISCELLANEOUS..5

    ADELINE.. 5

    The Sick Chamber... 14

    "Better laugh than cry."... 15

PREAMBLE..17

RESOLUTIONS..29

AFFIDAVITS..34

THE EXPOSITOR: INTRODUCTORY...37

JOE. SMITH - THE PRESIDENCY..47

TO CORRESPONDENTS...50

CIRCUIT COURT...52

CITIZENS OF HANCOCK COUNTY...54

TO THE VOTERS OF HANCOCK COUNTY....................................58

MR. EDITOR,...59

PENMANSHIP-Editors Note..61

ADMINISTRATOR'S SALE...61

NOTICE...62

PENMANSHIP..62

WARREN & HIGBEE...64

SONG...65

PHILADELPHIA RIOTS..66

The Papacy and the Great Powers...69

THE MORMONS...70

[NOTE FROM THE UPPER MISSISSIPPIAN]...................................72

THE JEWS IN RUSSIA.. 73

ANECDOTE OF THE MAYOR OF TIVERTON...............................74

EXTRACT FROM "GEN. SMITH'S VIEWS"..................................... 76

PROSPECTUS OF THE NAUVOO EXPOSITOR...............................80

TERMS...83

PRINTERS AND BINDERS WAREROOMS.......................................84

THE NEW MIRROR...85

UNPARALLELED SUCCESS... 87

WEEKLY DOLLAR MESSAGE... 87

ON DESTROYING THE NAUVOO EXPOSITOR...............................90

THE 'NAUVOO EXPOSITOR'

is published on Friday of each week,

and furnished to subscribers on the following terms:

$2.00 per annum, in advance,

$2.50 at the expiration of six months,

$3.00 at the end of the year.

Six copies will be forwarded to one address for

Ten Dollars in advance;

Thirteen copies for Twenty Dollars, &c.

ADVERTISEMENTS

For One Square, or under,	$1.00
For each continuance,	0.50

A liberal deduction made to yearly advertisers.

[ORIGINAL] PUBLISHERS

WILLIAM LAW,

WILSON LAW,

CHARLES IVINS,

FRANCIS M. HIGBEE,

CHAUNCEY L. HIGBEE,

ROBERT D. FOSTER,

CHARLES A. FOSTER.

POETRY

The Last Man
BY THOMAS CAMPBELL

All worldly shapes shall meet in gloom,
   The sun himself shall die,
Before this mortal shall assume
   Its immortality!
I saw a vision in my sleep,
   That gave my spirit strength to sweep
Adown the gulf of time!
   I saw the last of human mold,
That shall creation's death behold,
   As Adam saw her prime!

The sun's eye had a sickly glare,
   The earth with age was wan;
The skeletons of nations were
   Around that lonely man!
Some had expired in flight,—the brands
   Still rusted in their bony hands!
In plagues and famine some!
   Earth's cities had no sound nor tread;
And ships were drifting with the dead
   To shores where all was dumb!

Yet prophet like, that lone one stood,
   With dauntless words and high,
That shook the sere leaves from the wood
   As if a storm pass'd by,—
Saying, "We are twins in death proud Sun
   Thy face is cold, thy race is run,
'Tis mercy bids thee go.
   For thou ten thousand thousand years
Hast seen the tide of human tears,
   That shall no longer flow.

"What though beneath thee man put forth,
   His pomp, his pride his skill;
And arts that made fire, flood, and earth,
   The vassals of his will;
Yet mourn I not thy parted sway,
   Thou dim, discrowned king of day:
For all those trophied arts
   And triumphs that beneath thee sprang,
Healed not a passion or a pang
   Entail'd on human hearts.

"Go, let oblivion's curtain fall
   Upon the stage of men;
Nor with thy rising beams recall
   Life's tragedy again.
Its piteous pageants bring not back
   Nor waken flesh, upon the rack
Of pain anew to writhe;
   Stretch'd in disease's shape s abhorr'd.
Or mown in battle by the sword,
   Like grass beneath the scythe.

"Ev'n I am weary in yon skies
    To watch thy fading fire;
Test of all sunless agonies,
    Behold me not expire.
My lips that speak thy dirge of death,
    Their rounded grasp and gurgling breath,
To see thou shalt not boast.
    The eclipse of nature spreads my pall,
The majesty of darkness shall
    Receive my parting ghost!

"This spirit shall return to him!
    That gave its heavenly spark;
Yet think not Sun, it shall be dim
    When thou thyself art dark!
No it shall live again, and shine
    In bliss unknown to beams of thine,
By Him recall'd to breath,
    Who captive led captivity,
Who robbed the grave of victory,
    And took the sting from Death!

"Go, Sun, while mercy holds me up
    On nature's awful waste,
To drink this last and bitter cup
    Of grief that man shall taste;
Go, tell the night that hides thy face,
    Thou saw'st the last of Adam's race,
On earth's sepulchral clod;
    The dark'ning universe defy
To quench his immortality,
    Or shake his trust in God!"

ADELINE
Or, The Two Suitors

It was on a beautiful evening in summer, when, as the evening sun was hiding his red disk behind the distant mountains, and nature seemed sinking to a sweet repose, a horseman was jogging at a gentle pace down a lane, which led to the quiet village of E— . He was a young man of about two and twenty, and with the ladies, might have passed for a tolerably handsome man. By the appearance of his horse he had been riding fast, which was pretty clearly accounted for in the following exclamation, which fell from him as he slackened his pace:

"To-morrow, then," cried he, joyfully, "to-morrow shall I be united to the lovely being, in whose hands now rests my future happiness—to-morrow!"

But here his musings were interrupted by the clatter of horses' hoofs, approaching at a swift pace behind him, and the next moment a horseman, muffled in a large cloak, reined up his steed, with a powerful jerk, at his side. They rode on for some distance in silence, until Henry, for that was our hero's name, addressed him with—

"A fine evening, sir!"

"It is," answered the stranger—whose features and accent denoted him to be a foreigner—"It is very fine." Then, after a pause he continued: "Being a stranger in this country, I should feel obliged, sir, if you would direct me to the village of E—."

"Willingly," replied Henry; "it is to E— that I am going, and, if I shall not intrude, shall be happy to accompany you."

The stranger expressed his thanks, and, after a short time resumed:

"I suppose you reside in E—, sir?"

"Why, not exactly a resident, but rather a frequent visitor, as you may suppose," answered the light-hearted Henry, "when I tell you that the magnet which attracts me is a lady."

"And by such a magnet," replied the stranger, with a sigh, "I have been drawn from the sunny shores of Italy; attend awhile, and, in return for your confidence, you shall hear my story, and during its relation, our horses will cool:

"About a year ago, there came to Naples an old gentleman with his wife, who was an invalid, and a lovely daughter. They engaged a villa near the one in which I resided; I, thereby, became acquainted with the gentleman, who invited me to his house; but as his daughter was constantly in attendance on her mother, I never could meet her. I called again and again for the same purpose, but was as often disappointed, until shortly after, the old lady dying, I, with some other neighbors, was invited to the funeral. I saw her then in all the loveliness of woman's sorrow, bending over her mother's grave, and thought that I had never beheld a being so beautiful.

From that moment I loved her, and resolved to solicit her hand. After waiting to allow her grief to subside, I called, and finding her alone, at once told her the state of my feelings regarding her; but she, with apparent grief for my disappointment, firmly rejected my advances. They quitted Naples suddenly, and I have not seen them since, but have followed them hither with the intention of again preferring my suit."

"And if, when you have found her, she is engaged to another?"

The stranger's brow darkened, and his eyes flashed fiercely, as he exclaimed, "It should *not be!* This hand would deprive *him* of the happiness denied to *me.*"

"What! would you reduce the woman you loved to misery?"

"Young man, you know not the fiery pangs of rejected love; or, at least, we, sons of the South, are warmer in such matters than you of this colder clime."

"Well, well! I wish you success, and will, if you allow me, mention your case to a friend at E—, in whose house I shall sleep; probably he will be able to assist you in your search; by-the-bye, De Moncey has been in Italy, so I have no doubt will be delighted to have you for his guest; but here is the village. I will conduct you to the inn, as I intend leaving my horse there."

The start given by the stranger, together with the ashy paleness which overspread his features, at the mention of the name of "De Moncey," were unnoticed by the gay and unsuspecting Henry, who, spurring his horse, cantered gaily on to the inn.

"De Moncey!" ejaculated the stranger. "Ha! this is well, my search is ended—but can it be De Moncey's daughter to whom this gallant speeds? For *his* sake, I hope not; that, however, I must ascertain."

They had now arrived at the inn, when Henry, having alighted, walked on to the house of De Moncey, promising to call on the stranger early the next morning.

The road to the mansion lay up an avenue of nearly a mile in length, and shaded on each side by a thick row of tall pines. He had now reached the house, and was proceeding to the door, when the tinkling of a guitar, in the garden, caught his ear. Guessing who was the musician, he entered the garden, and stealing behind a bower, he beheld, through the leaves, his beloved Adeline seated with her guitar.

He could refrain no longer, but rushing into the bower, clasped her to his breast. The blush which overspread her face at being thus caught, was dispelled by the joy of beholding him in whom her earthly happiness was centered.

"Now, I declare," said Adeline, playfully tapping his shoulder, "that you have become quite a truant! I have not seen you for more than *a whole day*."

"Sweetest," replied Henry, embracing her, "you must forgive me; I staid but to settle some affairs *now*, that I might not again be torn from you—though I must confess that I should have been here earlier but for a companion I picked up on the road; nay, look not so hardly, Adeline, it was a *man*, and if you heard his story, you would, I have no doubt, forgive him the delay he caused *me*—but you shall hear it some other time."

Adeline, however, would rather hear it *then*. Henry, therefore, related the story of the stranger, and looking at Adeline, as he concluded, was surprised to find her in tears.

"Dearest Adeline," exclaimed he, taking her hand, "let it not affect you thus; he will, I dare say, be made happy, as you will make *me* to-morrow."

"Henry," replied Adeline, with a deep sigh, "I am more concerned in this unhappy tale than you imagine; I have reason for supposing that I am the female of whom he is in search."

"You! Adeline?"

"I have not mentioned this before, lest you should think me vain, but I will tell you now. You already know, my dear Henry, that my mother, being in a bad state of health, by the physician's advice, we went to reside at Naples. When we had been there but a short time, my father formed an acquaintance with an Italian nobleman, who, on the death of my mother, made me an offer in marriage; but, notwithstanding his wealth and handsome person, I felt that I could not love him, even if *you* had not already possessed my affections. On my rejection of his offer, he left the house in anger, and I did not see him again."

"'Tis strange—so exactly does it coincide—yet, Adeline, this *may* not be he."

"I hope not; still, I cannot but think it is."

"And if it is," said Henry, fixing his eyes searchingly upon her, "and *he* should repeat his offers?"

The eyes of Adeline, beaming with an expression of confidence, innocence and love, replied—"Yours till death."

He would have clasped her in his arms; but, at the instant, a rustling in the bushes near them caused them both to start from their seats. Adeline, greatly terrified, clung to her lover; who, after a time, hearing nothing else, attempted, though vainly, to calm her fears; but she begged him to conduct her into the house, which request he very reluctantly complied with.

Passing through one of the rooms, they encountered the father of Adeline, who, having a pretty shrewd guess at the locality of Henry during the preceding hour, *at least*, did not think it necessary to inquire the cause of his late arrival. Before they entered the drawing-room, where the guests who had been invited to the wedding were assembled, Adeline begged Henry to acquaint her father with the story of the stranger. The old man appeared as much struck with the coincidence as his daughter had been; but seeing its effect upon her, promised to visit E— in the morning, and if the stranger should prove to be the Italian, spare her the pain of an interview.

This arranged, they entered the drawing-room, where, in the pleasure of the evening the melancholy of Adeline was dispelled, and the stranger and his story alike forgotten.

*　　*　　*　　*　　*

When Henry awoke the next morning, the sun was shining brightly into his chamber, and the wild little vocalists without, chirping their merry songs of greeting to the day. He arose with the fondest anticipations of happiness; and hastily dressing, descended to the garden, where he found De Moncey already awaiting him. Thinking it the best time for their visit to E—, they set out for that place, and were much surprised on arriving to learn that the stranger had already departed, whither they could not learn; but the man who had taken his horse on the preceding evening, informed them that, on Henry's departure from the inn, "the strange gentleman had been moighty 'quisitive zurely; for," said he, "he axed me all about yer honer and miss, and whether or noa there war'nt nobody as paid his 'dresses to her; so I up un told um that as how I b'lieved so, and that there was a weddin up there this morning. Lord love you, sir, he look'd the colour o' old white Peggy there, till I thought the mon war gone crazy; but he starts off all at once towards yer honer's house; so I thought, maybe, he was an old friend, and war in order 'cause yer honer didn't ax him to the wedding."

"Well, my good fellow, did he not say anything at starting, this morning?"

"Oh, he war as grumpy as may be, an' only ax'd the nearest way to the sea, so I told un the *nearest*, which, yer honer knows, lays *clean over the cliff.*"

De Moncey could not help smiling at the oddity of the direction; and, rewarding the man for his information, they returned home.

"I have no longer any doubt, Henry, by the inquiries that he made, that it was my Italian friend, who, on finding the hopelessness of the case, and moreover that you, to whom he seems to have taken a liking, were his rival, has departed in despair."

They had now reached the house, when Henry, espying his beloved in the garden, ran to acquaint her with the result of their walk. She was greatly relieved by the news; and, with light hearts, they entered the breakfast-room. The breakfast was soon dispatched, and the joyous party set out on their journey to the church, which was situate at one end of the park, through which, as the cavalcade passed, it was saluted-by the glad shouts of the assembled tenantry, whose merry faces bore witness of the general joy, and added additional pleasure to the good De Moncey.

They had now arrived at the church; and the happy bridegroom handing out his blushing bride, they proceeded gaily up the little path which led to the door. In passing through the porch, Adeline slightly trembled. Henry stopped to kiss her hand; and, in an instant, a dagger from behind pierced him to the heart.

He fell, and, murmuring "Adeline," expired. The bereaved one, uttering a piercing shriek, fell senseless on the body of her beloved. The spectators, horror-struck, stood gazing vacantly at each other, until they were aroused by a voice in the crowd, crying "Seize him, seize him!"

Turning, they beheld a figure rush along the path; and, springing on a horse tied up near the gate, dash off at full speed. Every one rushed simultaneously out, and mounting every horse they could find, started in pursuit. They pursued for some time, gaining rapidly on the fugitive, until he turned up a short lane, which terminated in a terrific precipice.

"Hold! hold!" shouted the foremost of the pursuers, as they turned into the lane. "Would you follow him over the cliff?"

"He must be dashed over before he can stop his horse." A sharp cry of terror announced the truth of the prediction, and all was silent.

In deep silence, each meditating on the events of the morning, they returned to the church, where they had left De Moncey and his daughter. The scene which presented itself was heartrending in the extreme. The bereaved bride, not yet recovered from her swoon, was still extended on the lifeless body of Henry; the old man bending over this wreck of his fond hopes, absorbed in a sorrow too deep for tears.

They bore with them the body of Henry back to the mansion of De Moncey, where, after a time, Adeline recovered. But to what did she recover? Better, far better, had she have died. It was too evident that, with the spirit of her lover, her reason had fled forever. Her father was, from that hour, never seen to smile. The cup of happiness, so cruelly snatched from his lips, had left him a heart-broken man.

———

The Sick Chamber

Health and the Sun have been always sung and praised; I will now celebrate sickness and shade. I will celebrate thee, bodily sickness, when thou layest thy hand on the head and heart of man, and sayest to the sufferings of his spirit, 'Enough!'

Thou art called on earth an evil; oh! how often art thou a good, a healing balsam, under whose benign influence the soul rests after its hard struggles, and its wild storms are still! More than once hast thou prevented suicide, and preserved from madness.

The terrible, the bitter words which destroy the heart, are by degrees obliterated during the feverish dreams of illness; the terrors which lately seemed so near us are drawn away into the distance; we forget—God be thanked—we forget! and when at last we arise with exhausted strength from the sick-bed, our souls often awake as out of a long night into a new morning.

So many things, during the illness of the body, conspire to soften the feelings; the still room; the mild twilight through the window curtains; the low voices; and then, more than all, the kind words of those who surround us; their attention, their solicitude, perhaps a tear in their eyes; all this does us good; and when the wise Solomon enumerated all the good things which have their time upon the earth, he forgot to celebrate sickness among the rest.

———

"Better laugh than cry."

—So say we. It's no use rubbing one's eyes, and blubbering over all "the ills that flesh is heir to." Red eyes caused by anything but grief or its kindred are scandalous looking affairs. The best way is to "stand up to the rack," and take the good things and the evil as they come along, without repining; and always cheering yourself with that philosophical ejaculation, "better luck next time."

Is dame fortune as shy as a weasel? Tell her to go to thunder, and laugh her in the face. The happiest fellow we ever saw, slept upon a plank—and hadn't a shilling in his pocket, nor a coat to his back.

Do you find "disappointment lurking in many a prize?" Then throw it away, and laugh at your own folly for pursuing it.

Does fame elude your grasp? Then laugh at the fools that are so often her favorites. She's of no consequence any how, and never buttered a piece of bread or furnished a man a clean dickey.

Is your heart broken by

"Some maiden fair,

Of bright blue eyes and auburn hair?"

Then thank your stars that you have escaped with your neck, and make the welkin ring with a hearty laugh. It lightens the weight of one's heart amazingly.

Take our advice under all circumstances; "drive dull care away." Don't be in a hurry to get out of the world, considering the creatures who inhabit it, and it is just about as full of fun as it can be. You never saw a man cut his throat with a broad grin on his face; it's a grand preventative of suicide. There's philosophy and religion too, in laughing; it shows a clear conscience and gratitude for the good things of life, and elevates us above the brute creation. So here goes for fun—and we'll put in for our share while the ball is rolling, ha! ha!!

————

We give place this week to the following Preamble, Resolutions and Affidavits, of the Seceders from the Church at Nauvoo.— The request is complied with on account of their deeming it very important that the public should know the true cause of their dissenting, as all manner of falsehood is spread abroad in relation to the schism in the Church. In our subsequent numbers several affidavits will be published, to substantiate the facts alleged. Hereafter, no further Church proccedings will appear in our columns, except in the form of brief communications.—ED. [ORIGINAL EDITOR]

PREAMBLE

IT is with the greatest solicitude for the salvation of the Human Family, and of our own souls, that we have this day assembled. Feign would we have slumbered, and "like the Dove that covers and conceals the arrow that is preying upon its vitals," for the sake of avoiding the furious and turbulent storm of persecution which will gather, soon to burst upon our heads, have covered and concealed that which, for a season, has been brooding among the ruins of our peace: but we rely upon the arm of Jehovah, the Supreme Arbiter of the world, to whom we this day, and upon this occasion, appeal for the rectitude of our intentions.

If that God who gave bounds to the mighty deep, and bade the ocean cease—if that God who organized the physical world, and gave infinity to space, be our front guard and our rear ward, it is futile and vain for man to raise his puny arm against us. God will inspire his ministers with courage and with understanding to consummate his purposes; and if it is necessary, he can snatch them from the fiery furnace, or the Lion's den; as he did anciently the three Hebrews from the former, and Daniel from the latter.

As for our acquaintance with the Church of Jesus Christ of Latter Day Saints, we know, no man or set of men can be more thoroughly acquainted with its rise, its organization, and its history, than we have every reason to believe we are. We all verily believe, and many of us know of a surety, that the religion of the

Latter Day Saints, as originally taught by Joseph Smith, which is contained in the Old and New Testaments, Book of Covenants, and Book of Mormon, is verily true; and that the pure principles set forth in those books, are the immutable and eternal principles of Heaven, and speaks a language which, when spoken in truth and virtue, sinks deep into the heart of every honest man.

Its precepts are invigorating, and in every sense of the word, tend to dignify and ennoble man's conceptions of God and his attributes. It speaks a language which is heard amidst the roar of Artillery, as well as in the silence of midnight: it speaks a language understood by the incarcerated spirit, as well as he who is unfettered and free; yet to those who will not see, it is dark, mysterious, and secret as the grave.

We believe that all men, professing to be the ministers of God, should keep steadily in view, the honor and glory of God, the salvation of souls, and the amelioration of man's condition: and among their cardinal virtues ought to be found those of faith, hope, virtue and charity; but with Joseph Smith, and many other official characters in the Church, they are words without any meanings attached—worn as ornaments; exotics nurtured for display; virtues which, throwing aside the existence of a God, the peace, happiness, welfare, and good order of society, require that they should be preserved pure, immaculate and uncorroded.

We most solemnly and sincerely declare, God this day being witness of the truth and sincerity of our designs and statements, that happy will it be with those who examine and scan Joseph Smith's pretensions to righteousness; and take counsel of human affairs, and of the experience of times gone by. Do not yield up tranquilly a superiority to that man which the reasonableness of past events, and the laws of our country declare to be pernicious and diabolical. We hope many items of doctrine, as now taught, some of which, however, are taught secretly, and denied openly, (which we know positively is the case,) and others publicly, considerate men will treat with contempt; for we declare them heretical and damnable in their influence, though they find many devotees. How shall he, who has drank of the poisonous draft, teach virtue? In the stead thereof, when the criminal ought to plead guilty to the court, the court is obliged to plead guilty to the criminal. We appeal to humanity and ask, what shall we do? Shall we lie supinely and suffer ourselves to be metamorphosed into beasts by the Syren tongue? We answer that our country and our God require that we should rectify the tree. We have called upon him to repent, and as soon as he shewed fruits meet for repentance, we stood ready to seize him by the hand of fellowship, and throw around him the mantle of protection; for it is the salvation of souls we desire, and not our own aggrandizement.

We are earnestly seeking to explode the vicious principles of Joseph Smith, and those who practice the same abominations and whoredoms; which we verily know are not accordant and consonant with the principles of Jesus Christ and the Apostles; and for that purpose, and with that end in view, with an eye single to the glory of God, we have dared to gird on the armor, and with God at our head, we most solemnly and sincerely declare that the sword of *truth* shall not depart from the thigh, nor the buckler from the arm, until we can enjoy those glorious privileges which nature's God and our country's laws have guaranteed to us— freedom of speech, the liberty of the press, and the right to worship God as seemeth us good.

We are aware, however, that we are hazarding every earthly blessing, particularly property, and probably life itself, in striking this blow at tyranny and oppression: yet notwithstanding, we most solemnly declare that no man, or set of men combined, shall, with impunity, violate obligations as sacred as many which have been violated, unless reason, justice and virtue have become ashamed and sought the haunts of the grave, though our lives be the forfeiture.

Many of us have sought a reformation in the church, without a public exposition of the enormities of crimes practiced by its leaders, thinking that if they would hearken to counsel, and shew fruit meet for repentance, it would be as acceptable with God, as though they were exposed to public gaze,

"For the private path, the secret acts of men,

If noble, for the noblest of their lives."

but our petitions were treated with contempt; and in many cases the petitioner spurned from their presence, and particularly by Joseph, who would state that if he had sinned, and was guilty of the charges we would charge him with, he would not make acknowledgment, but would rather be damned; for it would detract from his dignity, and would consequently ruin and prove the overthrow of the Church. We would ask him on the other hand, if the overthrow of the Church was not inevitable, to which he often replied, that we would all go to Hell together, and convert it into a heaven, by casting the Devil out; and says he, Hell is by no means the place this world of fools suppose it to be, but on the contrary, it is quite an agreeable place: to which we would now reply, he can enjoy it if he is determined not to desist from his evil ways; but as for us, and ours, we *will* serve the Lord our God!

It is absurd for men to assert that all is well, while wicked and corrupt men are seeking our destruction, by a perversion of sacred things; for all is *not* well, while whoredoms and all manner of abominations are practiced under the cloak of religion. Lo! the wolf is in the fold, arrayed in sheep's clothing, and is spreading death and devastation among the saints: and we say to the watchmen standing upon the walls, cry aloud and spare not, for the day of the Lord is at hand—a day cruel both with wrath and fierce anger, to lay the land desolate.

It is a notorious fact, that many females in foreign climes, and in countries to us unknown, even in the most distant regions of the Eastern hemisphere, have been induced, by the sound of the gospel, to forsake friends, and embark upon a voyage across waters that lie stretched over the greater portion of the globe, as they supposed, to glorify God, that they might thereby stand acquitted in the great day of God Almighty. But what is taught them on their arrival at this place?

They are visited by some of the Strikers, for we know not what else to call them, and are requested to hold on and be faithful, for there are great blessings awaiting the righteous; and that God has great mysteries in store for those who love the Lord, and cling to brother Joseph. They are also notified that brother Joseph will see them soon, and reveal the mysteries of Heaven to their full understanding, which seldom fails to inspire them with new confidence in the Prophet, as well as a great anxiety to know what God has laid up in store for them, in return for the great sacrifice of father and mother, of gold and silver, which they gladly left far behind, that they might be gathered into the fold, and numbered among the chosen of God.

They are visited again, and what is the result? They are requested to meet brother Joseph, or some of the Twelve, at some insulated point, or at some particularly described place on the bank of the Mississippi, or at some room, which wears upon its front— *Positively NO admittance.* The harmless, inoffensive, and unsuspecting creatures, are so devoted to the Prophet, and the cause of Jesus Christ, that they do not dream of the deep laid and fatal scheme which prostrates happiness, and renders death itself desirable, but they meet him, expecting to receive through him a blessing, and learn the will of the Lord concerning them, and what awaits the faithful follower of Joseph, the Apostle and Prophet of God, when in the stead thereof, they are told, after having been sworn in one of the most solemn manners, to never divulge what is revealed to them, with a penalty of death attached, that God Almighty has revealed it to him, that she should be his (Joseph's) Spiritual wife; for it was right anciently, and God will tolerate it again: but we must keep those pleasures and blessings from the world, for until there is a change in the government, we will endanger ourselves by practicing it – but we can enjoy the blessings of Jacob, David, and others, as well as to be deprived of them, if we do not expose ourselves to the law of the land. She is thunder-struck, faints, recovers, and refuses. The Prophet damns her if she rejects. She thinks of the great sacrifice, and of the many thousand miles she has traveled over sea and land, that she might save her soul from pending ruin, and replies, God's will be done, and not mine. The Prophet and his devotees in this way are gratified.

The next step to avoid public exposition from the common course of things, they are sent away for a time, until all is well; after which they return, as from a long visit. Those whom no power or influence could seduce, except that which is wielded by some individual feigning to be a God, must realize the remarks of an able writer, when he says, "if woman's feelings are turned to ministers of sorrow, where shall she look for consolation?" Her lot is to be wooed and won; her heart is like some fortress that has been captured, sacked, abandoned, and left desolate. With her, the desire of the heart has failed—the great charm of existence is at an end; she neglects all the cheerful exercises of life, which gladden the spirits, quicken the pulses, and send the tide of life in healthful currents through the veins. Her rest is broken. The sweet refreshment of sleep is poisoned by melancholy dreams; dry sorrow drinks her blood, until her enfeebled frame sinks under the slightest external injury. Look for her after a little while, and you find friendship weeping over her untimely grave; and wondering that one who but so recently glowed with all the radiance of health and beauty, should so speedily be brought down to darkness and despair, you will be told of some wintry chill, of some casual indisposition that laid her low! But no one knows of the mental malady that previously sapped her strength, and made her so easy a prey to the spoiler. She is like some tender tree, the pride and beauty of the grove—graceful in its form, bright in its foliage, but with the worm praying at its heart; we find it withered when it should be most luxuriant. We see it drooping its branches to the earth, and shedding leaf by leaf until wasted and perished away, it falls in the stillness of the forest; and as we muse over the beautiful ruin, we strive in vain to recollect the blast or thunderbolt that could have smitten it with decay. But no one knows the cause except the foul fiend who perpetrated the diabolical deed.

Our hearts have mourned and bled at the wretched and miserable condition of females in this place; many orphans have been the victims of misery and wretchedness, through the influence that has been exerted over them, under the cloak of religion and afterwards, in consequence of that *jealous disposition* which predominates over the minds of *some*, have been turned upon a wide world, fatherless and motherless, destitute of friends and fortune; and *robbed of that which nothing but death can restore.*

Men solace themselves by saying the facts slumber in the dark caverns of midnight. But Lo! it is sudden day, and the dark deeds of foul fiends shall be exposed from the house-tops. A departed spirit, once the resident of St. Louis, shall yet cry aloud for vengeance.

It is difficult—perhaps impossible— to describe the wretchedness of females in this place, without wounding the feelings of the benevolent, or shocking the delicacy of the refined; but the truth shall come to the world. The remedy can never be applied, unless the disease is known. The sympathy, ever anxious to relieve, cannot be felt before the misery is seen.

The charity that kindles at the tale of wo, can never act with adequate efficiency, till it is made to see the pollution and guilt of men, now buried in the death-shades of heathenism.

Shall we then, however painful the sight, shrink from the contemplation of their real state? We answer, we will not, if permitted to live. As we have before stated, it is the vicious principles of men we are determined to explode. It is not that we have any private feelings to gratify, or any private pique to settle, that has induced us to be thus plain; for we can respect and love the criminal, if there is any hope of reformation: but there is a point beyond which forbearance ceases to be a virtue.

The next important item which presents itself for our consideration, is the attempt at Political power and influence, which we verily believe to be preposterous and absurd. We believe it is inconsistent, and not in accordance with the christian religion. We do not believe that God ever raised up a Prophet to christianize a world by political schemes and intrigue. It is not the way God captivates the heart of the unbeliever; but on the contrary, by preaching truth in its own native simplicity, and in its own original purity, unadorned with anything except its own indigenous beauties. Joseph may plead he has been injured, abused, and his petitions treated with contempt by the general government, and that he only desires an influence of a political character that will warrant him redress of grievances; but we care not—the faithful followers of Jesus must bear in this age as well as Christ and the Apostles did anciently; although a frowning world may have crushed him to the dust; although unpitying friends may have passed him by; although hope, the great comforter in affliction, may have burst forth and fled from his troubled bosom; yet, in Jesus there is a balm for every wound, and a cordial to assuage an agonized mind.

Among the many items of false doctrine that are taught the Church, is the doctrine of *many Gods*, one of the most direful in its effects that has characterized the world for many centuries. We know not what to call it other than blasphemy, for it is most unquestionably, speaking of God in an impious and irreverent manner.

It is contended that there are innumerable Gods as much above the God that presides over this universe, as he is above us; and if he varies from the law unto which he is subjected, he, with all his creatures, will be cast down as was Lucifer; thus holding forth a doctrine which is effectually calculated to sap the very foundation of our faith: and now, O Lord! shall we set still and be silent, while thy name is thus blasphemed, and thine honor, power and glory, brought into disrepute? See Isaiah c 43, v 10; 44, 6-8; 45, 5, 6, 21, 22; and book of Covenants, page 26 and 39.

In the dark ages of Popery, when bigotry, superstition, and tyranny held universal sway over the empire of reason, there was some semblance of justice in the inquisitorial deliberations, which, however, might have been dictated by prudence, or the fear of consequences: but we are no longer forced to appeal to those states that are now situated under the influence of Popery for examples of injustice, cruelty and oppression—we can appeal to the acts of the inquisitorial department organized in *Nauvoo*, by Joseph and his accomplices, for specimens of injustice of the most pernicious and diabolical character that ever stained the pages of the historian.

It was in Rome, and about the twelfth century, when Pope Innocent III, ordered father Dominic to excite the Catholic princes and people to extirpate heretics. But it is in this enlightened and intelligent nineteenth century, and in Nauvoo--a place professing to be the nucleus of the world, that Joseph Smith has established an inquisition, which, if it is suffered to exist, will prove more formidable and terrible to those who are found opposing the iniquities of Joseph and his associates, than even the Spanish inquisition did to heretics as they termed them.

On Thursday evening, the 18th of April, there was a council called, unknown to the Church, which tried, condemned, and cut off brothers Wm. Law, Wilson Law, and sister Law, (Wm's. wife,) brother R. D. Foster, and one brother Smith, with whom we are unacquainted; which we contend is contrary to the book of Doctrine and Covenants, for our law condemnest no man until he is heard. We abhor and protest against any council or tribunal in this Church, which will not suffer the accused to stand in its midst and plead their own cause. If an Agrippa would suffer a Paul, whose eloquence surpassed, as it were, the eloquence of men, to stand before him, and plead his own cause, why should Joseph, with others, refuse to hear individuals in their own defense?

We answer, it is because the court fears the atrocity of its crimes will be exposed to public gaze. We wish the public to thoroughly understand the nature of this court, and judge of the legality of its acts as seemeth them good.

On Monday, the 15th of April, brother R. D. Foster had a notice served on him to appear before the High Council on Saturday following, the 20th, and answer to charges preferred against him by Joseph Smith. On Saturday, while Mr. Foster was preparing to take his witnesses, 41 in number, to the council-room, that he might make good his charges against Joseph, president Marks notified him that the trial had been on Thursday evening, before the 15th, and that he was cut off from the Church; and that same council cut off the brother Laws', sister Law, and brother Smith, and all without their knowledge. They were not notified, neither did they dream of any such thing being done, for William Law had sent Joseph and some of the Twelve, special word that he desired an investigation before the Church in General Conference, on the 6th of April. The court, however, was a tribunal possessing no power to try Wm. Law, who was called by special Revelation, to stand as counselor to the President of the Church, (Joseph,) which was twice ratified by General Conferences, assembled at Nauvoo, for Brigham Young, one of the Twelve, presided, whose duty it was not, but the President of the High Council.— See Book of Doctrine and Covenants, page 87.

———

RESOLUTIONS

Resolved 1st, That we will not encourage the acts of any court in this church, for the trial of any of its members, which will not suffer the accused to be present and plead their own cause; we therefore declare our decided disapprobation to the course pursued last Thursday evening, (the 18th inst,) in the case of William and Wilson Law, and Mrs. William Law, and R. D. Foster, as being unjust and unauthorized by the laws of the Church, and consequently null and void; for our law judgeth no man unless he be heard; and to all those who approbate a course so unwarranted, unprecedented and so unjust, we would say beware lest the unjust measure you mete to your brethren, be again meted out to you.

Resolved 2nd, Inasmuch as we have for years borne with the individual follies and iniquities of Joseph Smith, Hyrum Smith, and many other official characters in the Church of Jesus Christ, (conceiving it a duty incumbent upon us so to bear,) and having labored with them repeatedly with all Christian love, meekness and humility, yet to no effect, feel as if forbearance has ceased to be a virtue, and hope of reformation vain; and inasmuch as they have introduced false and damnable doctrines into the Church, such as a plurality of Gods above the God of this universe, and his liability to fall with all his creations; the plurality of wives, for time and eternity; the doctrine of unconditional sealing up to eternal life, against all crimes except that of shedding innocent blood, by a perversion of their priestly authority, and thereby forfeiting the holy priesthood, according to the word of Jesus; "If a man abide not in me, he is cast forth as a branch and is withered, and men gather them and cast them into the fire, and they are burned," St. John, xv. 6. "Whosoever transgresseth and abideth not in the doctrine of Christ, hath not God, he that abideth in the doctrine of Christ, hath both the Father and the Son; if there come any unto you and bring not this doctrine, receive him not into your house, neither bid him God speed, for he that bideth him God speed is a partaker of his evil deeds;" we therefore are constrained to denounce them as apostates from the pure and holy doctrines of Jesus Christ.

Resolved 3rd, That we disapprobate and discountenance every attempt to unite church and state; and that we further believe the effort now being made by Joseph Smith for political power and influence, is not commendable in the sight of God.

Resolved 4th, That the hostile *spirit* and *conduct* manifested by Joseph Smith, and many of his associates towards Missouri, and others inimical to his purposes, are decidedly at variance with the true spirit of Christianity, and should not be encouraged by any people, much less by those professing to be the ministers of the gospel of peace.

Resolved 5th, That while we disapprobate malicious persecutions and prosecutions, we hold that all church members are alike amenable to the laws of the land; and that we further discountenance any chicanery to screen them from the just demands of the same.

Resolved 6th, That we consider the religious influence exercised in financial concerns by Joseph Smith, as unjust as it is unwarranted, for the Book of Doctrine and Covenants makes it the duty of the Bishop to take charge of the financial affairs of the Church, and of all temporal matters pertaining to the same.

Resolved 7th, That we discountenance and disapprobate the attendance at houses of reveling and dancing; dram-shops and theaters; verily believing they have a tendency to lead from paths of virtue and holiness, to those of vice and debauchery.

Resolved 8th, That we look upon the pure and holy doctrines set forth in the Scriptures of Divine truth, as being the immutable doctrines of salvation; and he who abideth in them shall be saved, and he who abideth not in them can not inherit the Kingdom of Heaven.

Resolved 9th, That we consider the gathering in haste, and by sacrifice, to be contrary to the will of God; and that it has been taught by Joseph Smith and others for the purpose of enabling them to sell property at most exorbitant prices, not regarding the welfare of the Church, but through their covetousness reducing those who had the means to give employment to the poor, to the necessity of seeking labor for themselves; and thus the wealth which is brought into the place is swallowed up by the one great throat, from whence there is no return, which if it had been economically dispersed amongst the whole would have rendered all comfortable.

Resolved 10th, That, notwithstanding our extensive acquaintance with the financial affairs of the Church, we do not know of any property which in reality belongs to the Church (except the Temple) and we therefore consider the injunction laid upon the saints compelling them to purchase property of the Trustee in trust for the Church, is a deception practiced upon them: and that we look upon the sending of special agents abroad to collect funds for the Temple and other purposes as a humbug practiced upon the saints by Joseph and others, to aggrandize themselves, as we do not believe that the monies and property so collected, have been applied as the donors expected, but have been used for speculative purposes, by Joseph, to gull the saints the better on their arrival at Nauvoo, by buying the lands in the vicinity and selling again to them at tenfold advance; and further that we verily believe the appropriations said to have been subscribed by shares for the building of the Nauvoo House to have been used by J. Smith and Lyman Wight, for other purposes, as out of the mass of stock already taken, the building is far from being finished even to the base.

Resolved 11th, That we consider all secret societies, and combinations under penal oaths and obligations, (professing to be organized for religious purposes,) to be anti-Christian, hypocritical and corrupt.

Resolved 12th, That we will *not* acknowledge any man as king or law-giver to the church; for Christ is our only king and law-giver.

Resolved 13th, That we call upon the honest in heart, in the Church, and throughout the world, to vindicate the pure doctrines of Jesus Christ, whether set forth in the Bible, Book of Mormon, or Book of Covenants; and we hereby withdraw the hand of fellowship, from all those who practice or teach doctrines contrary to the above, until they cease so to do, and show works meet for repentance.

Resolved 14th, That we hereby notify all those holding licenses to preach the gospel, who know they are guilty of teaching the doctrine of other Gods above the God of this creation; the plurality of wives; the unconditional sealing up against all crimes, save that of shedding innocent blood; the spoiling of the gentiles, and all other doctrines, (so called) which are contrary to the laws of God, or to the laws of our country, to cease preaching, and to come and make satisfaction, and have their licenses renewed.

Resolved 15th, That in all our controversies in defense of truth and righteousness, the weapons of our warfare are not carnal but mighty through God, to the pulling down of the strongholds of Satan; that our strifes are not against flesh, blood, nor bones; but against principalities and power against spiritual wickedness in high places and therefore we will not use carnal weapons save in our own defense.

———

AFFIDAVITS

I hereby certify that Hyrum Smith did, (in his office,) read to me a certain written document, which he said was a revelation from God, he said that he was with Joseph when it was received. He afterwards gave me the document to read, and I took it to my house, and read it, and showed it to my wife, and returned it next day. The revelation (so called) authorized certain men to have more wives than one at a time, in this world and in the world to come. It said this was the law, and commanded Joseph to enter into the law.

And also that he should administer to others. Several other items were in the revelation, supporting the above doctrines.

WM. LAW.

State of Illinois

Hancock County

I, Robert D. Foster, certify that the above certificate was sworn to before me, as true in substance, this fourth day of May A D 1844.

ROBERT D. FOSTER, J. P.

I certify that I read the revelation referred to in the above affidavit of my husband, it sustained in strong terms the doctrine of more wives that one at a time, in this world, and in the next, it authorized some to have to the number of ten, and set forth that those women who would not allow their husbands to have more wives than one should be under condemnation before God.

JANE LAW

Sworn and subscribed before me this fourth day of May, AD 1844.

ROBERT D. FOSTER, J. P.

To all whom it may Concern:

Forasmuch as the public mind hath been much agitated by a course of procedure in the Church of Jesus Christ of Latter Day Saints, by a number of persons declaring against certain doctrines and practices therein, (among whom I am one,) it is but meet that I should give my reasons, at least in part, as a cause that hath led me to declare myself.

In the latter part of the summer, 1843, the Patriarch, Hyrum Smith, did in the High Council, of which I was a member, introduce what he said was a revelation given through the Prophet; that the said Hyrum Smith did essay to read the said revelation in the said Council, that according to his reading there was contained the following doctrines; 1st. the sealing up of persons to eternal life, against all sins, save that of shedding innocent blood or of consenting thereto; 2nd, the doctrine of a plurality of wives, or marrying virgins; that "David and Solomon had many wives, yet in this they sinned not save in the matter of Uriah. This revelation with other evidence, that the aforesaid heresies were taught and practiced in the Church, determined me to leave the office of first counselor to the president of the Church at Nauvoo, inasmuch as I dared not teach or administer such laws. And further deponent saith not.

AUSTIN COWLES

State of Illinois

Hancock County

To all whom it may concern, I hereby certify that the above certificate was sworn and subscribed before me, this fourth day of May, 1844.

ROBERT D. FOSTER, J. P.

———

THE EXPOSITOR:
INTRODUCTORY

FRIDAY, JUNE 7, 1844

SYLVESTER EMMONS, EDITOR

In greeting our patrons with the first number of the Expositor, a remark is necessary for the expression of some views, and certain principles by which we intend to be governed in our editorial duties. Many questions and surmises are made by those who suppose we will come in conflict with some of their darling schemes of self-aggrandizement.

Others, more honest, desire to know whether our object is to advocate any particular religious tenets, or any favorite measures of either of the political parties of the country. To all such questions we answer in the negative. Free toleration in religious sentiments, we deem compatible with the organization of our government, and should not be abridged.

On the other hand, we believe religious despotism to be incompatible with our free institutions. What we conceive to be despotism, engendered by an assumption of power in the name of religion, we shall have occasion to show hereafter. In relation to politics, whatever our own views may be upon the federal measures that now, or may, hereafter agitate the country, the Expositor will not be the exponent thereof; and all the strife and party zeal of the two great antagonistical parties for the success of their respective candidates for the Presidency, we shall remain neutral, and in an editorial capacity, inactive.

Another party, however, has sprung up in our midst, the leader of which, it would seem, expects, by a flourish of Quixotic chivalry, to take, by storm, the Presidential chair, and distribute among his *faithful* supporters, the office of governor in all the different States, for the purpose, we presume, of more effectually consolidating the government. This party we may be disposed to treat with a little levity, but nothing more.

As it respects the local questions which may arise in our own county, and the candidates for the legislature from this county, we reserve the right to expatiate upon the respective claims—not on account of their politics—be they whig or democrat, but on account of a combination which we believe has for its object the utter destruction of the rights of the old citizens of the county, who have borne the heat and burden of the day; who have labored hard as pioneers of the county; who have settled and organized the county; who have rights that should be respected by every principle of honor and good faith, and whose wishes should be consulted in the choice of officers, and not have men imposed upon them, who are obnoxious, for good and sufficient reasons.

In relation to such questions, we intend to express our mind freely, as our duty dictates, regardless of consequences. If a fair and honorable course be taken by the dominant party at Nauvoo, we will have nothing to battle against; but if they do not pursue that course, we shall be prepared for the warfare. We must confess, however, if we are to judge of the future by the past, we have little to expect from that quarter: but apart from local political considerations, we have a high and more noble duty to perform.

We shall spread the banner to the breeze for a radical reform in the city of Nauvoo, as the departure from moral rectitude, and the abuse of power, have become intolerable. We shall speak out, and spare not, until certain grievances are redressed or corrected; until honor, virtue, and reputation shall take their accustomed habitations, and be respected; until we teach men that no exclusive privileges can be allowed to any individual under our form of government; that the law of the land, based upon the revealed laws of heaven, are paramount to all other earthly considerations; and he who sets the laws at defiance, and evades their operation, either by direct or indirect means, pursues a course subversive of the best interests of the country, and dangerous to the well-being of the social compact. That there does exist an order of things with the systematic elements of organization in our midst—a system which, if exposed in its naked deformity, would make the virtuous mind revolt with horror; a system in the exercise of which lays prostrate all the dearest ties in our social relations—the glorious fabric upon which human happiness is based—ministers to the worst passions of our nature, and throws us back into the benighted regions of the dark ages, we have the greatest reason to believe.

The question is asked, will you bring a mob upon us? In answer to that, we assure all concerned that we will be among the first to put down anything like an illegal force being used against any man or set of men. If any one has become amenable to the law, we wish to have him tried impartially by the laws of his country. We are among the number who believe that there is virtue and integrity enough in the administrators of the law, to bring every offender to justice, and to protect the innocent.

If it is necessary to make a show of force, to execute legal process, it will create no sympathy in that case to cry out, 'we are mobbed'. There is such a thing as persons being deceived into a false sympathy once, who, the second time, will scrutinize very closely, to know who, or which party, are the persecutors. It is not always the first man who cries out, 'stop thief', that is robbed. It is the upright, honest, considerate and moral precepts of any class that will be respected in this or any other enlightened age— precepts which have for their end the good of mankind, and the establishment of fundamental truths.

On the other hand, paradoxical dogmas, new systems of government, new codes of morals, a new administration of the laws by ignorant, unlettered, and corrupt men, must be frowned down by every lover of his country. The well-being of society demands it at our hands. Our country, by whose laws we are protected, asks us for a manifestation of that patriotism which should inspire every American citizen—the interests of the State of Illinois require it, and as a citizen of Illinois, we intend to respond to the voice of duty, and stand the hazard of the die.

We believe that the Press should not be the medium through which the private character of any individual should be assailed, delineated, or exposed to public gaze: still, whoever acts in an official character, who sets himself up as a public teacher, and reformer of morals and religion, and as an aspirant to the highest office in the gift of the people of this glorious republic, whose institutions he publicly condemns, we assert and maintain the right of canvassing all the public acts and animadverting, with terms of the severest reproach upon all the revolutionary measures that comes to our notice, from any source.

We would not be worthy of the name of an American citizen, did we stand by and see, not only the laws of the State, but the laws of the United States set at defiance, the authorities insulted, fugitives from justice fleeing for refuge, asking and receiving protection from the authorities of Nauvoo, for high crimes committed against the government of the United States, the Mayor of a petty incorporated town interposing his authority, and demanding the right of trial for the fugitive on the merits of the case, by virtue of a writ of *Habeas Corpus*, issued by the Municipal Court of Nauvoo. It is too gross a burlesque upon common sense—a subterfuge too low to indicate anything but a corrupt motive.

Such acts, whether committed in a private or public capacity, will be held up to public scorn. An independent Press is bound by every sense of duty, to lay before the public every attack upon their rights: we, therefore, in the exercise of our duty, expect the support and the aid of our fellow citizens in our enterprise.

———

We hope all those who intend subscribing for the "Expositor," will forward their names as soon as possible; Editors, Postmasters, and others, to whom the Prospectus, and paper may be sent, will confer a favor upon us, by noticing, exchanging, and circulating the same, in their respective vocations, and forwarding accordingly.

In consequence of the importance of the cause in which we have engaged, and the assurances we have received from different sources, we have concluded to issue one thousand copies of the first number of the paper, that all who wish, may be supplied, and further, that none may plead ignorance of our complaints, or exonerate themselves from an interest in our behalf.

We do not wish, or expect, the publication of the "Expositor" to prove a matter of pecuniary profit, neither do we believe the public will suffer it to prove a loss. It is a subject in which we are all interested, more particularly the citizens of this county, and surrounding country; the case has assumed a formidable and fearful aspect, it is not the destiny of a few that is involved in case of commotion, but that of thousands, wherein necessarily the innocent and helpless would be confounded with the criminal and guilty. We have anxiously desired, and strenuously advocated a peaceable redress of the injuries that have repeatedly been inflicted upon us, and we have now the means in our hands, through which we can peaceably and honorably effect our object. For ourselves, we are firmly resolved not to quit the field, till our efforts shall be crowned with success. And we now call upon all, who prize the liberty of speech, the liberty of the press, the right of conscience, and the sacred rights of American citizenship, to assist us in this undertaking. Let us stand up and boldly and fearlessly oppose ourselves to any and every encroachment, in whatever form it may appear, whether shaped in superstitious domination or civil usurpation. The public abroad have not been informed in relation to facts as they really existed in our midst, many have supposed that all was rumor, and having no organ through which to speak, our silence has been to them sufficient proof.

The facts have been far otherwise, we have watched with painful emotion the progress of events in this city, for some time past, until we were sick with the sight; injury upon injury has been repeated, insult has been added to insult till forbearance has ceased to be virtuous, and we now have the proud privilege we have long wished for, of defending ourselves against their foul aggressions and aspersions and of informing the public of things as they really are.

We intend to tell the whole tale and by all honorable means to bring to light and justice, those who have long fed and fattened upon the purse, the property, and the character of injured innocence;—yes, we will speak, and that too in thunder tones, to the ears of those who have thus ravaged and laid waste fond hopes, bright prospects, and virtuous principles, to gratify an unhallowed ambition. We are aware of the critical position we occupy, in view of our immediate location; but we entertain no fears, our purpose is fixed and our arm is nerved for the conflict, we stand upon our rights, and we will maintain those rights, whatever may be the consequence; let no man or set of men assail us at the peril of their lives, and we hereby give notice to all parties, that we are the last in attack, but the first and foremost in defense. We would be among the last to provoke the spirit of the public abroad unnecessarily, but we have abundant assurance, in case of emergency, that we shall be all there.

———

An individual, bearing the cognomen of Jeremiah Smith, who has evaded the officers for some time, has taken refuge in the city of Nauvoo. It appears he is a fugitive from justice for the offense of procuring four thousand dollars from the United States Treasury at the city of Washington, under false pretenses. A bill of indictment was found in the District of Columbia against him, and a warrant issued for his arrest.

The Marshal of Iowa Territory got intelligence of his being in this place, and procuring the necessary papers for his arrest, proceeded to this place in search of him, about three weeks ago. After making inquiry, and becoming satisfied that he was secreted in Nauvoo, under the immediate protection of the Prophet, he said to him (the Prophet,) that he was authorized to arrest the said J. Smith, for an offense committed by him against the United States government, and wished to know where he was—to which the Prophet replied, that he knew nothing about him. The Marshal said he knew he was secreted in the city, and was determined to have him; and, unless he was given up, he would have the aid of the Dragoons to find and arrest him. Joseph Smith then replied, that was not necessary; but, if the Marshal would pledge his word and honor that he should have the benefit of a city writ of *Habeas Corpus*, and be tried before him, he would produce the fugitive in half an hour.

After some hesitancy, the Marshal agreed to do so, when the prisoner was produced in the time specified. A writ of *Habeas Corpus* was issued, and the prisoner taken from the Marshal and brought before the Municipal court of Nauvoo for trial. The court adjourned until thursday, the 30th ult., when he was tried, and discharged, as a matter of course. In the interval, however, application had been made to Judge Pope, of the District court of the United States for the State of Illinois, who issued his warrant, directed to the United States Marshal, who sent his deputy to make a second arrest, in case the other officer did not succeed in taking him from the city. Smith was found by the Illinois Marshal and arrested, when it became necessary for the high corporate powers of the city again to interpose their authority. The potent writ was again issued—the prisoner taken from the Marshal—a trial had, during which, the attorneys for Smith relieved themselves of an insupportable burthen of legal knowledge, which completely overwhelmed the learned court, and resulted in the triumphant acquittal of the prisoner, with a judgment for costs against the U. States.

Now we ask if the executive and judicial authorities of Illinois deem it politic to submit to such a state of things in similar cases? Can, and will the constituted authorities of the federal government be quiescent under such circumstances, and allow the paramount laws of the Union to be set at defiance, and rendered nugatory by the action of a court, having no more than coordinate powers, with a common justice of the peace? If such an order of things is allowed to exist, there is every reason to believe that Nauvoo will become a sink of refuge for every offender who can carry in spoils enough to buy protection. The people of the State of Illinois will, consequently, see the necessity of repealing the charter of Nauvoo, when such abuses are practiced under it; and by virtue of said chartered authority, the right of the writ of *Habeas Corpus* in all cases arising under the city ordinance, to give full scope to the desired jurisdiction. The city council have passed ordinances, giving the Municipal court authority to issue the writ of *Habeas Corpus* in all cases when the prisoner is held in custody in Nauvoo, no matter whether the offender is committed in the State of Maine, or on the continent of Europe, the prisoner being in the city under arrest. It is gravely contended by the legal luminaries of Nauvoo, that the ordinances gives them jurisdiction, not only jurisdiction to try the validity of the writ, but to enquire into the merits of the case, and allow the prisoner to swear himself clear of the charges. If his own oath is not considered sufficient to satisfy the adverse party, plenty of witnesses are ready to swear that he is to be believed on oath, and that is to be considered sufficient by the court to put the quietus on all foreign testimony and the discharge of the prisoner follows, as a necessary consequence.

———

JOE. SMITH - THE PRESIDENCY

We find in the *Nauvoo Neighbor* of May 29th, a lengthy letter from Joseph Smith, a candidate for the Presidency on his own hook, to Henry Clay, the Whig candidate for the same office. It appears to be a new rule of tactics for two rival candidates to enter into a discussion of their respective claims to that high office, just preceding an election. Smith charges Clay with shrinking from the responsibility of promising to grant whatever the Mormons might ask, if elected to the Presidency.

Smith has not been troubled with any inquiries of committees as to what measures he will recommend if elected; nevertheless he has come out boldly and volunteered his views of certain measures which he is in favor of having adopted. One is for the General Government to purchase the slaves of the south and set them free, that we can understand. Another is to pass a general uniform land law, that certainly requires the spirit of interpretation to show its meaning as no explanation accompanies it.

Another which no doubt will be very congenial to the candidate's nervous system, is to open all the prison doors in the country, and set the captive free. These with some other suggestions equally as enlightened, ought to be sufficient to satisfy any man that Joseph Smith is willing that his principles shall be publicly known. If however, any individual voter, who has a perfect right to know a candidate's principles, should not be satisfied, he may further aid his inquiries, by a reference to the record to the grand inquest of Hancock County.

Martin Van Buren is charged with non-commitalism; Henry Clay has not been the man to answer frankly the question whether he would restore to the Mormons their lands in Missouri. Joseph Smith is the only candidate now before the people whose principles are fully known; let it be remembered there are documents the highest degree of evidence before the people; a committee of twenty-four, under the solemnity of their oaths, have inquired into and reported upon his claims in due form of law. Shades of Washington and Jefferson—Henry Clay, the candidate of a powerful party, is now under bonds to keep the peace; Joseph Smith, the candidate of another *"powerful"* party has two indictments against him, one for fornication and adultery, another for perjury. Our readers can make their own comments.

———

We have received the last number of the *"Warsaw Signal;"* it is rich with anti-Mormon matter, both editorial and communicated. Among other things it contains a lengthy letter from J. H. Jackson, giving some items in relation to his connection with the *"Mormon Prophet,"* as also his reasons for the same. It will be perceived that many of the most dark and damnable crimes that ever darkened human character, which have hitherto been to the public, a matter of *rumor* and *suspicion*, are now reduced to *indisputable facts*.

We have reason to believe, from our acquaintance with Mr. Jackson, and our own observation, that the statements he makes are true; and in view of these facts, we ask, in the name of heaven, where is the safety of our lives and liberties, when placed at the disposal of such heaven daring, hell deserving, God forsaken villains. Our blood boils while we refer to these blood thirsty and murderous propensities of men, or rather *demons* in human shape, who, not satisfied with practicing their dupes upon a credulous and superstitious people, must wreak their vengeance upon any who may dare to come in contact with them.

We deplore the desperate state of things to which we are necessarily brought, but, we say to our friends, *"keep cool,"* and the *whole tale* will be told. We fully believe in bringing these iniquities and enormities to light, and let the majesty of violated law, and the voice of injured innocence and contemned public opinion, speak in tones of thunder to these miscreants; but in behalf of hundreds and thousands of unoffending citizens, whose only fault is religious enthusiasm, and for the honor of our own names and reputation, let us not follow their desperado measures, and thereby dishonor ourselves in revenging our own wrongs. Let our motto be, "Last in attack, but first in defense;" and the result cannot prove otherwise than honorable and satisfactory.

———

TO CORRESPONDENTS

In consequence of a press of other duties in preparing our first number for the press, we have not had time to examine several communications that have been forwarded for publication. We respect the motives of our friends in the interest they manifest in carrying forward the work of reform; but we wish it to be distinctly understood, that we cannot depart from the conditions set forth in the Prospectus; that is the chart by which we intend to navigate the "Expositor," carefully avoiding anything and everything that may tend to diminish the interest, or tarnish the character of its columns. We already feel that we occupy an unenviable position in view of the variety of opinions that exist, but, we stand committed as to our course, and having faithfully and fearlessly adhered to those terms, without partiality to friends, or personality to foes, we shall consider ourselves honorably discharged of duty.

———

We offer an apology to our readers for the want of arrangement and taste in our first number on account of our materials and press not being in order; the short time we have had to get a press and materials has precluded the possibility of getting the first number out according to our wishes, and the absence of the Editor for several days preceding our first issue, renders this apology necessary. In our subsequent numbers we intend to make good the insufficiency by giving to our readers a good selection of miscellany, and an editorial of rich and interesting matter.

PROPRIETORS

———

CIRCUIT COURT

The May Term of the Circuit Court of this county closed on the 30th ult. after a session of ten days. We understand a large number of cases were disposed of, none, however of a very important character. The cases wherein Joseph Smith was a party, were transferred by a change of venue, to other courts; that of A. Sympson vs. J. Smith, for false imprisonment, to Adams County; that of F. M Higbee vs. Joseph Smith, for slander, and that of C. A. Foster vs. Joseph Smith, and J. W. Coolidge for false imprisonment, and that of A. Davis vs. Joseph Smith, and J. P. Green, for trespass, were all transferred to the County of McDonough. The Grand Jury found two bills against Smith, one for perjury, and another for fornication and adultery; on the first of which Smith delivered himself up for trial, but the State not being ready, material witnesses being absent, the case was deferred to the October term.

———

The regular session of the Municipal Court of this City came off on Monday last. The cases of R. D. Foster, C. L. Higbee, and C. A. Foster, on appeals from the Mayor's Court, wherein they had each been fined in the sum of one hundred dollars, (for the *very enormous* offense of refusing to assist the notorious O. P.

Rockwell, and his '*dignity*' John P. Green, in arresting a respectable and peaceable citizen, without the regular process of papers)
and of A. Spencer, wherein he was fined in the same sum on a
charge of assault and battery, were all taken up and gravely
discussed; after the most mature deliberation, with the assistance
of the *ex*-tinguished City Attorney, this honorable body concluded
to dismiss the suit and issue a *procedendo* to the lower court, which
was accordingly done.

The cases referred to above, afford abundant reason both
for complaint and comment. We intend as soon as our time will
allow, to express our views fully and freely upon this feature of
Mormon usurpation; first, enact a string of ordinances contrary to
reason and common sense, and then inflict the severest penalties
for not observing them.

————

We see that our friend the *Neighbor* advocates the claims of
Gen. Joseph Smith for the Presidency; we also see from the records
of the grand Jury of Hancock Co. at their recent term, that the
general is a candidate to represent the branch of the state
government at Alton. We would respectfully suggest to the
Neighbor, whether the two offices are not incompatible with each
other.

————

CITIZENS OF
HANCOCK COUNTY

NAUVOO JUNE 5th, 1844

It is well known to all of you that the August election is fast approaching, and with it comes the great and terrible conflict. It is destined to be a day pregnant with big events; for it will be the index to the future.

Should we be defeated upon that occasion, our die is cast, and our fate is sealed; but if successful, alike may Joseph Smith, Hyrum Smith, and their devoted followers, as well as their enemies, expect that justice will be meted out. The present is portentous of the great effort that is to be made upon that occasion, by Joseph for power; Hiram Smith is already in the field as a candidate for the legislature, but will you support *him*, that same *Hyrum Smith* the devoted follower and brother of Joe, who feigned a revelation from God, directing the citizens of Hancock County to vote for J. P. Hoge, in preference to Cyrus Walker, and by so doing blaspheming the name of God?

Will *you*, gentlemen of Hancock County, support a man like that, who claims to move in a different sphere, a sphere entirely above you; one who will trifle with the things of God, and feign converse with the Divinity, for the sake of carrying an election? I will unhesitatingly assume to myself the responsibility of answering in the negative. I flatter myself you are not so depraved, and so blinded to your own interests, as to support a man totally ignorant of the laws of your country, and in every respect alienated from you and your interests.

In supporting *Hyrum Smith*, you, *Citizens of Hancock County*, are supporting Joseph Smith, for whom he (Hyrum) goes teeth and toenails, for President of the United States. The question may arise here, in voting for Joseph Smith, for whom am I voting? You are voting for a man who contends all governments are to be put down and the *one* established upon its ruins. You are voting for an *enemy* to your government.

Hear Phelps to Joe in his affidavit before Judge King of Missouri:—"Have you come to the point to resist all law?"

"I have," says Joe.

You are voting for a sycophant, whose attempt for power finds no parallel in history. You are voting for a man who refuses to suffer criminals to be brought to justice, but in the stead thereof, rescues them from the just demands of the law, by *Habeas Corpus.* You are voting for a man who stands indicted, and who is now held to bail, for the crimes of adultery and perjury; two of the gravest crimes known to our laws. Query not then for whom you are voting; it is for one of the blackest and basest scoundrels that has appeared upon the stage of human existence since the days of Nero, and Caligula.

In supporting Hyrum Smith, then are you not supporting Joseph Smith? most assuredly; pause then, my *countrymen*, and consider cooly, calmly and deliberately, what you do? Support not

that man who is spreading death, devastation and ruin throughout your happy country like a tornado. Infinite are the gradations
which mark this man's attempts for power, which if not checked
soon, must not only shed a deleterious influence on the face of this
county, but on the face of the adjoining counties.

He is already proudly boasting that he is beyond your
reach; and I regret to think I am under the painful necessity of
admitting the fact. Is it not a shame and a disgrace, to think we
have a man in our midst, who will defy the laws of our country; the
laws which shed so gentle and nourishing an influence upon our
fathers, which fostered and protected them in their old age from
insult and aggression; shall we their sons, lie still and suffer *Joseph
Smith* to light up the lamp of tyranny and oppression in our midst?
God forbid, lest the departed spirits of our *fathers*, cry from the
ground against us. Let us arise in the majesty of our strength and
sweep the influence of tyrants and miscreants from the face of the
land, as with the breath of heaven. The eagle that is now proudly
borne to earth's remotest regions by every gale, will perch himself
in the solitude of midnight if we do not arouse from our lethargy.

It is the worst of absurdities for any individual to say there
is a man in our midst who is above the reach of violated law, and
not lend a helping hand; all talk and nothing more will not
accomplish *that* for your country and your God, which the acts of
Washington did. Then gentlemen organize *yourselves* and prepare
for the dreadful conflict in August; we go with you heart and hand,
in the attempt to suppress this contaminating influence which is

prostrating our fairest prospects, and spreading desolation throughout our vale.

Call into the field your best men under the solemn pledge to go for the unconditional repeal of the Nauvoo Charter, and you have our support; whether they be Whig or Democrat we care not; when a friend presents us with a draught of cool water, we do not stop to inquire whether it is contained in a silver vase, a golden urn or a long handled gourd. We want no base seducer, liar and perjured representative, to represent us in *Springfield*, but while Murrill represents Tennessee in Nashville, Munroe Edwards, New York, in Sing Sing, Br. Joseph may have the extreme goodness to represent Illinois in Alton, if his lawyers do not succeed in quashing the indictments found against him by the Grand Jurors of Hancock County, at the May term 1844.

FRANCIS M. HIGBEE

———

TO THE VOTERS OF
HANCOCK COUNTY

At the earnest request of a number of friends, I am induced to offer myself as a candidate for the office of Sheriff, at the ensuing August election. Should I be elected, I pledge myself to perform the duties incident to the office with independence and fidelity.

JOHN M. FINCH

Nauvoo, June 7th, 1844.--te

MR. EDITOR,

As I have taken some little interest in the affairs of the "Nauvoo Theatre;" I wish to announce through the medium of your paper, that the establishment, which left this place a few weeks since to travel, has again arrived in this city. What success the concern met with while absent I am unable to learn; the only thing of interest which I have been able to discover, is that the Rev. G. J. Adams was hissed from the stage in Burlington, while telling the "woodchuck story." I understand that the establishment has closed for the present, in consequence of Mr. Adams being under the necessity of 'going a preaching;' probably the Rev. Gentleman thinks by this time that he is better fitted for the desk than the stage.

I am Sir,
A FRIEND TO THE DRAMA

———

PENMANSHIP—We invite the attention of our readers to the advertisement of Mr. A. R. Dunton, found in another column of today's paper. We have examined several specimens of this Gentleman's handiwork, in the execution of his various style of penmanship, and we cheerfully award to him the merit of excelling anything of the kind in this department. Mr. Dunton brings with him testimonials of the highest character, from the most respectable sources; having borne off the palm of victory in several of our eastern cities;—but, aside from our own opinion, or the opinion of others, Mr. Dunton presents the best evidence, in his off hand efforts, which he executes with a neatness and dispatch that dispels all doubt, and wins for him the wreath of merited fame.— ED. [ORIGINAL EDITOR]

———

MARRIED:—At Carthage, on the 23d ult., by E. A. Bedell Esq. Mr. Charles Ross of St. Louis, to Miss Sabra A. Morrison, of this city. We tender our congratulations to the above parties upon their union of heart and hand, and express our warmest wishes for their future happiness.

———

ONE CENT REWARD—WHEREAS my husband, the Rt. Rev. W. H. Harrison Sagers, Esq., has left *my* bed and board without cause or provocation, this is to notify the public not to harbor or trust him on my account, as I will pay no debts of his contracting. More anon.

LUCINDA SAGERS

June 7, 1844.-tf.

ADMINISTRATOR'S SALE

ON the 20th of June, A D 1844, will be offered at public sale at the New Brick Store of S. M. Marr, on Knight Street, east of the Temple in the City of Nauvoo, the following described property, to wit: Household and kitchen furniture, consisting of beds and bedding, wearing apparel, cotton cloth, &c.

AUGUSTINE SPENCER

Administrator

Nauvoo, June 7th, 1844.--ltf.

NOTICE

THE Subscribers wish to inform all those who through sickness; or other misfortunes, are much limited in their means of procuring *bread* for their families, that we have allotted Thursday of every week, to grind TOLL FREE for them, till grain becomes plentiful after harvest.

P. S. Elder Cowles, or Bishop Ivins, will attend at our mill on those days set apart, and will judge very benevolently, in all cases where the above indulgence is claimed.

W. & W. LAW

Nauvoo, June 7th, 1844.--tf

PENMANSHIP

THOSE wishing to improve, the present very favorable opportunity for taking Lessons in *Penmanship,* and *Stylographic Card Marking,* are informed that the above branches will be taught by Mr. A. R. Dunton, in a manner that cannot fail to prove satisfactory to all. The system he teaches has no superior, either in acquisition, facility of execution, or elegance and uniformity of the letters.

Mr. D. would beg leave to refer the Ladies and Gentlemen of this City and its vicinity, to the fact that he has borne off the

FIRST PREMIUM for the *best Specimens of Penmanship* from all competitors, at the late Mechanics' Fair held in Boston.

Mr. Dunton proposes to award the following premiums, viz:

The person who shall make the best improvement in writing, shall be entitled to a specimen of penmanship worth from five to ten dollars. And if any person will produce a specimen superior to what Mr. D. will execute, the person producing it shall be entitled to fifty dollars.

For the best improvement in Stylographic Card Marking, the person shall be entitled to their tuition.

N. B. The above Premiums are to be awarded by a committee mutually chosen.

Those who have been disappointed by attending the Schools of incompetent teachers, are warranted perfect satisfaction at Mr. D's. School, or their money will be refunded.

Writing Masters fitted for the profession, Teachers, Professional, and Businessmen, and all good or bad writers, who wish to become complete masters of the art, are particularly invited to attend.

Writing rooms at the new Masonic Hall [on] Main St. Terms of tuition only $1,50 for 12 lessons. Classes will be formed on Monday evening next at 7 P. M.

June 7th, 1844.

———

SONG

The lads—I wonder how they guess it,
	I'm sure I never tell,
And *if* I love, I ne'er confess it—
	How can they guess so well?
I'm sure 'twas *no* I told my laddie—
	I would not love—not I;
He says 'twas *yes*, the saucy laddie!
	He saw *yes* in my eye.

My mother says 'tis naughty—very!
	For I am scarce fifteen;
I vowed, to please the dame so chary,
	My love should ne'er be seen.
And *still* 'twas *no* I told my laddie,
	And still—I wonder why?
He kissed me—ah, the saucy laddie!
	He saw love in my eye.

The love, I bade him tarry,
	Asleep, within my breast,
But when he heard my gentle Harry,
	The rebel would not rest.
And while I thought the boy was sleeping,
	Alack, he is so sly!
I found the rogue at Harry peeping,
	Ay, peeping through my eye.

———

[From the Philadelphia Times.]

PHILADELPHIA RIOTS

The Riots in Kensington—The Irish and the Native Americans

The late riots in Kensington between the Native Americans and the Irish Roman Catholics—for the feud is now a religious one entirely, conceal the fact as we may—have filled our city with excitement, and every thoughtful mind with deep reflection. What are we coming to? Are the people forgetting at once the elements of Republicanism, viz: tolerance of opinion, freedom of thought and action, and obedience to the laws, or can any man engaged in these disgraceful broils believe that he is aiding by such conduct, however provoked, in carrying out the principles of civil and religious liberty?

As a Protestant, and a Native born citizen, we protest against this unnatural admixture of religion and politics. In the whole history of the human race, we find the bloodiest pages those in which are recorded the contest of the Church; are we willing to introduce this firebrand of destruction and desolation into the midst of our peaceful and happy country? Have we a mind to rival Europe in our chronicles of inhuman massacre and slaughter, or shall we bathe our hearth-stones in blood, and make our homes charnel-houses, because of differences of opinion, the entertainment of which is guaranteed to every American citizen, whether Native-born or Naturalized by our glorious Constitution?

66

We are opposed to the political sentiments of the Native Americans, but we respect their sincerity, and would be the last to stand silently by and see them insulted; to see their peaceable assemblies broken up by an infuriated multitude, and see them or any other set of men, whether right or wrong in their views, waylaid and assaulted for promulgating their political notions. We are too much of a Republican, and have too much genuine American feeling for this; but, we are equally opposed to the introduction of religious abuse into political orations; we entertain a very contemptuous opinion of the wisdom, the law-and-order-loving disposition, and the *real* Christianity of those demagogues who do it to accomplish, by the fearful public orgasm which must follow, their own selfish ends.

We give up to no man in our respect for the Bible, and our zeal for its dissemination. We give up to no man in our love for our beloved country, its unparalleled institutions, its mighty and intelligent people, and above all its freedom from that curse of Europe, an union of Church and State. But, in tenaciously reserving for ourselves and our children the right to peruse the Bible, we should be the first to rebel against any attempt to coerce others into its perusal; in jealously watching to prevent the political dominance of any other religious persuasion, we should be among the first to denounce any attempt at such dominance contemplated by the members of our own.

These are the dictates of patriotism; nay more, they are the dictates of Christianity. Without pretending to take any side in this unfortunate controversy—without pretending that the Roman

Catholics are right or wrong, or that the Native Americans are right or wrong, for we conceive both to have committed a grievous error in appealing under any circumstances to physical force or to arms, —let us ask, is such conduct characteristic of either freemen or Christians? Is it the part of a true republican to thrust his opinions upon others, and to picture all those who differ from him as fit subjects for immolation; or did the great prototype of the Christian church when on the earth set his followers such a belligerent example? Was not the language of the later always "peace! peace?" Was not his course exemplarily specific? Did he turn even on his revilers and persecutors? Did he not take every occasion to teach his disciples forbearance, and radically subdue in them the slightest impulse towards retaliation?

If so, we are bound to follow the example as well as the advice of the head of the universal Christian church! And in doing so, we at once carry out the principles of good government, for republicanism and christianity are identical, and the very spirit of the one, is incorporated into and animates the other. Let us have *peace* then. Cease these wicked contentions. And in order that they may cease, stop at once this mingling together of religion and politics. Away with it. It is an unhallowed, iniquitous, and incestuous union. The issue must be a monster, misshapen and deplorable, inimical to liberty, repulsive to tranquil government, and ever associated with but anarchy, discord, murder, and civil war.

———

The Papacy and the Great Powers

The Tablet, a Catholic newspaper, takes a gloomy view of the present state of the Papal dominions, and the dangers which threaten them from several quarters. Amongst the most dangerous of these enemies is said to be Russia, whose Emperor is denounced as "the great Antichrist of the north," and from whose rule, when once it includes Italy, is predicted "a hideous persecution and calamity, such as the Church has never yet hardly witnessed."

The other enemies of the Papal see, besides its own insurgent subjects, are said to be England and France, and the following is a summary account of its alleged position at the present moment:

"Besides, then, the local and social convulsions of Italy, we have hanging over the Holy See---first, the armed Protectorate of Austria; secondly, the efforts of Russia to gain, at least, so much influence in Rome, as shall prevent the publication of unpleasant documents; thirdly, the endeavors of England to cajole the Pope into putting the screw (spiritual) upon his too ardent subjects in Ireland; and fourthly, the endeavors of France to secure the same advantage against the Catholic subjects of that kingdom.

The Pope, unable to uphold his temporal dominion without Austrian bayonets, and the three most powerful cabinets of Europe applying all their craft and force to compel his Holiness to abuse his spiritual power to the common injury of Christendom! Luckily, the hand of God has carried the Church through as great dangers as the present, and has promised to carry her through all dangers; otherwise we would say that this was no very pleasant prospect."

———

THE MORMONS

We last week gave some account of the dissensions and divisions which have sprung up in the holy city of Nauvoo—growing out of the arbitrary conduct of "the Prophet."

Since then, the breach has become still wider between the head of the church and his followers. The citizens have procured a press, and will soon commence a paper, for the purpose of exposing Smith on his own ground and among his own people.

Last week, individuals of the Mormon faith, (Messrs. Blakesley and Higbee,) representing the dissenters, addressed a large number of our citizens, in reference to the "flare up," at Nauvoo. We were not present, but have it from others who were, that the dissenters, made out that Joe Smith was pretty much of a rough customer, especially in relation to the "spiritual wife" doctrine. Their whole aim was principally against the church—of which they still claimed to be members. They painted Smith as anything but the saint he claims to be—and as a man, to the last degree, corrupt in his morals and religion.

On Wednesday night, Mr. John P. Green, a Mormon elder, addressed a crowded house in defense of "the Prophet." The principal portion of the worthy elder's speech, while we were in the house, was taken up, in an apology for addressing the meeting, and when he did come to the substance of his address, he could only disprove the statements made by the dissenters, from his own knowledge—he said he had been a Mormon for the last twelve years—and had always been intimate with Smith, and that such doctrines as were ascribed to Smith by his enemies, had never been taught to him. He further said that Smith was like a diamond, the more he was rubbed, the brighter he appeared—and he strongly insinuated that the characters of the individuals, who had assailed Smith on the second evening previous, were none of the best, &c.

We think these Mormon missionaries are laboring under a mistake in one particular. It is not so much the particular doctrines, which Smith upholds and practices, however abominable they may be in themselves, that our citizens care about—as it is the anti-republican nature of the organization, over which he has almost supreme control—and which is trained and disciplined to act in accordance with his selfish will. The spectacle presented in Smith's case of a civil, ecclesiastical and military leader, united in one and the same person, with power over life and liberty, can never find favor in the minds of sound and thinking Republicans.

The day has gone by when the precepts of Divine Truth could be propagated at the point of the sword—or the Bible made the medium of corrupt men to gratify their lustful appetites and sordid desires.

QUINCY WHIG

————

[NOTE FROM THE UPPER MISSISSIPPIAN]

We have received from Nauvoo a Prospectus for a new paper, to be entitled the *"Nauvoo Expositor."* It is intended to be the organ of the Reformed Mormon Church, which has lately been organized in that place, and to oppose the power of 'the self constituted Monarch,' who has assumed the government of the Holy City.

We care no more about the New Church than the Old one, as a church; for we regard both with indifference. But if it can be a means of humbling the haughty miscreant who rules in that city, and exposing his rank villanies, then we shall wish both Church and Paper a hearty Godspeed! The gentlemen who have the new paper in charge, have the reputation of being men of character and talent; and have commenced the work in which they are engaged, in real earnest. We hope the public will encourage their effort.

UPPER MISSISSIPPIAN

THE JEWS IN RUSSIA

A letter from St. Petersburg, dated March 21, says, that to check the emigration of the Jews over the frontiers, the following, sanctioned by the Emperor, had been made law;—"Jews who without legal licenses, or with legal licenses which have expired, go over the frontier, when they have before been recognized as actual Russian subjects, and as such been brought back into the empire, shall be given up to the local government authorities, who shall deal with them according to the laws relating to deserters and vagrants, even when the former places of residence and the parishes to which they belong are known. According to these laws, they shall be employed in the military service; in case they are unfit for it, be placed in what are called the penal companies, without the right of being given up to their parishes, if the latter shall desire it. If they are not fit for hard labor in the public works, they shall be sent with their wives to settle in Siberia."

———

ANECDOTE OF THE MAYOR OF TIVERTON

During the time when Wesley and Whitfield were gaining so many converts in many parts of England, the former came one day to preach at Tiverton.

This created considerable excitement in town, and the Mayor, fearing some riot might ensue, issued his proclamation, commanding Wesley to desist, as it was dangerous to the peace and good order that he should preach in that place. On being remonstrated with, he made the following laconic reply:

"I don't see what occasion there can be for any new religion in Tiverton! Why do we want another way of going to heaven when there is so many already? Why, sir, there's the old church and the new church, that's one religion; there's Parson Kiddell's at the Pitt meeting, that's two; Parson Wescott's, in Peter street, that's three; and old Parson Tarry's in Newport street, that's four. Four ways of going to heaven! If they won't go to heaven by one or the other of these ways, by——they shan't go to heaven at all from Tiverton, while I'm Mayor of the town."

————

THE AMERICAN PRESS AND THE REV. SYDNEY SMITH —The following letter from the pen of the Rev. Sydney Smith, has made its appearance in the *Morning Chronicle:*

To the Editor of the Chronicle:—

Sir—The loco-foco papers in America are, I observe, full of abuse of Mr. Everett, their minister for spending a month with me at Christmas, in Somersetshire. That month was neither lunar nor calendar, but consisted of forty-eight hours—a few minutes more or less.

"I never heard a wiser or more judicious defense than he made to me and others, of the American insolvency—not denying the injustice of it, speaking of it on the contrary, with the deepest feeling, but urging with great argumentative eloquence every topic that could be pleaded in extenuation. He made upon us the same impression he appears to make universally in this country; we thought him (a character which the English always receive with affectionate regard,) an amiable American republican, without ostentation. 'If I had known that gentleman five years ago, (said one of my guests,) I should have been deep in the American funds; and as it is, I think at times that I see nineteen shillings in the pound of his face.'

"However this may be, I am sure we owe to the Americans a debt of gratitude for sending to us such an excellent specimen of their productions. In diplomacy, a far more important object than falsehood, is to keep two nations in friendship. In this point, no nation has ever been better served than America has been served by Mr. Edward Everett.

"I am, sir, your ob't ser't,

SYDNEY SMITH

———

EXTRACT FROM "GEN. SMITH'S VIEWS"

"The people may have faults but they never should be trifled with. I think Mr. Pitt's quotation in the British Parliament of Mr. Prior's couplet for the husband and wife, to apply to the course which the king and ministry of England should pursue to the then colonies, of the *now* United States, might be a genuine rule of action for some of the *breath made* men in high places, to use towards the posterity of that noble daring people.

"Be to her faults a little blind;

Be to her virtues very kind."

"We have had democratic presidents; whig presidents; a pseudo democratic whig president: and now it is time to have *a president of the United States;* and let the people of the whole union, like the inflexible Romans, whenever they find a *promise* made by a candidate, that is not practiced as an officer, hurl the miserable sycophant from his exaltation, as God did Nebuchadnezzar, to crop the grass of the field, with a beast's heart among the cattle.

"Mr. Van Buren said in his inaugural address, that he went "into the presidential chair the inflexible and uncompromising opponent of Congress, to abolish slavery in the District of Columbia, against the wishes of the slave holding states; and also with a determination equally decided to resist the slightest interference with it in the states where it exists." Poor little Matty made his rhapsodical sweep with the fact before his eyes, that the state of New York, his native state, had abolished slavery, without a struggle or a groan. Great God, how independent!

From henceforth slavery is tolerated where it exists: constitution or no constitution; people or no people; right or wrong; vox Matti; vox Diaboli: "the voice of Matty"—"the voice of the devil;" and peradventure, his great "Sub-Treasury" scheme was a piece of the same mind: but the man and his measures have such a striking resemblance to the anecdote of the Welchman and his cart-tongue, that, when the constitution was so long that it allowed slavery at the capital of a free people, it could not be cut off; but when it was short that it needed a *Sub-Treasury*, to save the funds of the nation, *it could be spliced!* Oh, granny what a long tail our puss has got! As a Greek might say, *hysteron proteron;* the cart before the horse: but his mighty whisk through the great national fire, for the presidential chestnuts, *burnt the locks of his glory with the blaze of his folly!*

The above we extract from the celebrated state paper, entitled, "Gen. Smiths' views of the powers and policy of the Government of the United States," as a specimen of the original matter it contains.

With such astute penetrating views, such exalted and dignified sentiments, emanating from a candidate for the Presidency, Father Miller must be pronounced a humbug, and the people of the nineteenth century may look for the dawn of a glorious era to burst upon their astonished vision in the fall of eighteen hundred and forty-four, an era in which a Prophet only can tell whether granny's cat has a long tail or not; or whether the Greek's cart will be before the horse or otherwise; the constitution we presume will be as long as the Welchman's cart tongue, "peradventure" a little longer.

———

A Witty Reply. — When Mark Antony gave orders for doubling the taxes in Asia, an intimate friend of his told him, he should "first order the land to yield a double harvest."

———

A Queer Change. — The old spirit-stirring appeal to fight for your hearths, has become obsolete. It is now, "fight for your stoves and heaters!"

———

Not so Bad. — "I wish you had been Eve," said an urchin, to an old maid who was proverbial for her meanness.

"Why so?"

"Because," said he, "you would have eaten all the apple instead of dividing with Adam!"

———

Domestic Order. — We observe in the works of Madame Necker, what must be considered a good hint to housewives: "Domestic order, like theatrical machinery, produces the greatest pleasure when the strings are concealed."

———

Precious but Fragile. — The two most precious things on this side of the grave are reputation and life.--- But it is to be lamented that the most contemptible whisper may deprive us of the one, and the weakest weapon may deprive us of the other.

———

Father, what does the printer live on?

Why child?

You said you had not paid him for two or three years, and yet you have his paper every week!

Wife, put this child under the floor, he is too personal in his remarks.

———

PROSPECTUS
OF THE
NAUVOO EXPOSITOR

The undersigned propose publishing a Journal of the above title, which will appear on Friday of each week, on an Imperial sheet, with a new Press, and materials of the best quality, and rendered worthy of the patronage of a discerning and an enlightened public.

The Expositor will be devoted to a general diffusion of useful knowledge, and its columns open for the admission of all courteous communications of a Religious, Moral, Social, Literary, or Political character, without taking a decided stand in favor of either of the great Political parties of the country.

A part of its columns will be devoted to a few primary objects, which the Publishers deem of vital importance to the public welfare. Their particular locality gives them a knowledge of the many *gross abuses exercised under the pretended authorities of the Nauvoo City Charter,* by the legislative authorities of said city; and the insupportable *oppressions* of the *Ministerial* powers in carrying out the unjust, illegal, and unconstitutional ordinances of the same.

The publishers, therefore, deem it a sacred duty they owe to their country and their fellow citizens, to advocate, through the columns of the Expositor, the *UNCONDITIONAL REPEAL OF THE NAUVOO CITY CHARTER;* to restrain and correct the abuses of the *Unit Power;* to ward off the Iron Rod which is held over the devoted heads of the citizens of Nauvoo and the surrounding country; to advocate unmitigated *disobedience* to *Political Revelations,* and to censure and decry gross moral imperfections wherever found, either in the Plebian, Patrician, or *self-constituted MONARCH;* to advocate the pure principles of morality, the pure principles of truth; designed not to destroy, but strengthen the main-spring of God's moral government; to advocate, and *exercise,* the freedom of speech in Nauvoo, independent of the ordinances abridging the same; to give free toleration to every man's religious sentiments, and sustain all in worshiping God according to the monitions of their consciences, as guarantied by the Constitution of our country; and to oppose, with uncompromising hostility, any *Union of Church and State,* or any preliminary step tending to the same; to sustain all, however humble, in their equal and constitutional rights, and oppose the sacrifice of the Liberty, the Property, and the Happiness of the *many,* to the *pride* and *ambition* of the *few.*

In a word, to give a full, candid, and succinct statement of *facts, as they exist in the city of Nauvoo,* fearless of whose particular case they may apply, being governed by the laws of Editorial courtesy, and the inherent dignity which is inseparable from honorable minds; at the same time exercising their own judgment in cases of flagrant abuses, or moral delinquencies; to use such terms and names as they deem proper, when the object is of such high importance that the end will justify the means.

We confidently look to an enlightened public for aid in this great and indispensable effort.

The columns of the Expositor will be open to the discussion of all matters of public interest, the productions of all correspondents being subject to the decision of the Editor alone, who shall receive or reject at his option. National questions will be in place, but no preference given to either of the political parties. The Editorial department will contain the political news of the day, proceedings of Congress, election returns, &c., &c. Room will be given for articles on Agriculture, the Mechanic Arts, Commercial transactions, &c.

The publishers bind themselves to issue the paper weekly for one year, and forward fifty-two copies to each subscriber during the year. Orders should be forwarded as soon as possible, that the publishers may know what number of copies to issue.

The publishers take pleasure in announcing to the public that they have engaged the services of Sylvester Emmons, Esq., who will have entire charge and supervision of the editorial department. From an acquaintance with the dignity of character, and literary qualifications of this gentleman, they feel assured that the Nauvoo Expositor must and will sustain a high and honorable reputation.

———

TERMS

Two Dollars per annum in advance,

Two Dollars and Fifty cents at the expiration of six months,

Three Dollars at the end of the year.

Six copies will be forwarded to one address for Ten Dollars in advance; Thirteen copies for Twenty Dollars, &c.

Advertising and Job Work in all their varieties, done on short notice, and upon the most satisfactory terms.

All letters and communications must be addressed to *"Charles A. Foster, Nauvoo, Illinois,"* *post paid,* in order to insure attention.

Publishers:

William Law,

Wilson Law,

Charles Ivins,

Francis M. Higbee,

Chauncey L. Higbee,

Robert D. Foster,

Charles A. Foster

PRINTERS AND BINDERS WAREROOMS

—Nos. 29 and 31 Gold Street New York, April, 1844.—

Price Greatly Reduced—THE "HOE" PRINTING PRESS, MACHINE AND SAW MANUFACTORY, in consequence of the addition of new and improved machinery to their works and the reduction in the cost of materials and labor, are enabled greatly to reduce the prices of their presses and Printers and binders materials generally, as will be seen by their newly printed circular, to which they beg leave to refer.

This establishment is still under the personal superintendence of Richard M. Hoe and Robert Hoe, and they assure their friends that notwithstanding the great reduction in prices, all articles manufactured by this establishment shall retain the high reputation which they have hitherto sustained—It will also be their constant endeavor to improve the quality of them in every particular. They flatter themselves also, that their old friends will not only continue their favors, but that printers generally will appreciate their endeavors to furnish the very best articles at barely remunerating prices.

Orders from any part of the country for all articles by Printers and Binders, including Type, Ink, Paper, etc., will be executed with the greatest care and promptitude, and on the best terms.

Jobbing work and repairing will be done at the lowest possible prices, with every attention and expedition.

N. B.—All articles manufactured by this establishment will be stamped 'R. HOE & CO.', so that persons from abroad may not be imposed upon with *spurious* articles made in imitation of theirs.

Printers of Newspapers who publish this advertisement with this note, three times before the first of July next, and send one of their papers to us, will be entitled to payment on their bill on buying four times the amount of it.

THE NEW MIRROR

Every number embellished with an original and exquisite design on steel.

—

EDITED BY GEORGE P. MORRIS

—

Illustrated by J. C. CHAPMAN, who is engaged exclusively for the work.

TERMS---THREE DOLLARS PER ANNUM. Single numbers 6 1/4 cents.

In the course of a few weeks the undersigned will commence, on his own account, the publication of a *new series* of the *New York Mirror,* in the octavo form, on an entirely novel and original plan, with a steel engraving in every number and at the reduced price of three dollars per annum, or six and a quarter cents per copy.

The *New Mirror* will appear with many striking and attractive features, distinguishing it from every other periodical. It will be published with new type, on fine paper, and each number will contain a beautiful original engraving on steel, designed and etched by Chapman, illustrating the letterpress which it accompanies, and which it will invest with peculiar interest.

Besides the contributions of all our extensive corps of correspondents—which embraces most of the talent of this country—we have made arrangements for fresh and early translations from some of the best writers in France, and England. With such materials, and with such able fellow laborers in the literary vineyard, we hope to present to the American reader a weekly journal of great value and unusual excellence. The parade of mere names will be sedulously avoided.

The Mirror will be remarkable, we hope, rather for good articles without names, than for poor articles with distinguished names. It will embrace in its scope every department of elegant literature, comprising tales of romance, sketches of society and manners, sentiment, and everyday life, piquant essays, domestic and foreign correspondence, literary intelligence, wit and humor, fashion and gossip, poetry, the fine arts, and literary, musical and dramatic criticisms. Its reviews of new works will be careful, discriminating and impartial. It will aim to foster a literature suited to the taste and desires of the age and country. Its tendency will be cheerful and enlivening, as well as improving. It will seek to gratify every refined taste, but never to offend the most fastidious; and it will ever feel its duty to be, to "turn the sunny side of things to human eyes."

The work will be published every Saturday, in numbers of sixteen large octavo super royal pages, with double columns, and enclosed in a neat ornamental cover. It will form at the end of the year two superb volumes, each of four hundred and sixteen pages, filled with the gems of literature and the fine arts.

The very low price at which it will be issued, renders it the cheapest periodical in this or any other country.

UNPARALLELED SUCCESS
OF THE
WEEKLY DOLLAR MESSAGE

It is now nearly one year since the undersigned commenced the publication of the Weekly Dollar Message, a paper made up from the contents of the Daily Morning Message, which has been in existence nearly two years enjoying the best reputation of any paper in the Queen City for the early dissemination of intelligence and variety of interesting matter—comprising Literature, Poetry, Miscellany, the Current News of the day, Foreign and Domestic; carefully avoiding, however the least partisan bias in politics. It is equal in size and execution to any weekly in this city, containing a much larger amount of reading matter, and at the same time afforded at one half the price of the cheapest of them. It combines more completely than any of its Eastern rivals the distinguishing characteristics of a literary journal with those of a regular and systematic chronicle of passing events.

But the unparalleled patronage, from every section of the country, is the best evidence of its approval. The Weekly already has a circulation of over two thousand copies, and is increasing at the rate of from 50 to 100 per week.

For the best original Tale, not exceeding in length 30 pages of common foolscap manuscript, ONE HUNDRED DOLLARS,

And for the best original Poem, not exceeding 100 lines nor less than 50, THIRTY DOLLARS.

The Prize Tale and Poem to be published in the first No. of the 2nd vol., which will be issued on the 15th day of July next, at which time the prizes will be placed in the hands of the committee, subject to the orders of those to whom they may be awarded.

The following literary gentlemen have been appointed a committee, to whom the productions of all competitors for the above prizes will be submitted for decision, and from whose high standing in society, the most strict impartiality may be relied on:

ELAM P. LANGDON,

JAS H. PERKINS,

C. NICHOLS,

GEO. S. BENNETT,

JOSEPH McCLURE

ON DESTROYING THE
NAUVOO EXPOSITOR
[added by Edina Publishers for context]

"To the Marshal of said City, greeting.

You are here commanded to destroy the printing press from whence issues the Nauvoo Expositor, and pi the type of said printing establishment in the street, and burn all the Expositors and libelous handbills found in said establishment; and if resistance be offered to your execution of this order by the owners or others, demolish the house; and if anyone threatens you or the Mayor or the officers of the city, arrest those who threaten you, and fail not to execute this order without delay, and make due return hereon.

By order of the City Council,
Joseph Smith, Mayor"

- History of the Church, v. 6, p. 448

"General [Joseph] Smith…. I attribute the last outbreak to the destruction of the Expositor, and to you[r] refusal to comply with the writ issued by Esq. Morrison. The press in the United States is looked upon as the great bulwark of American Freedom, and its destruction in Nauvoo was resented and looked upon as a high-handed measure, and manifests to the people a disposition on your part to suppress the liberty of speech and of the press; this, with your refusal to comply with the requisition of a writ, I conceive to be the principal cause of this difficulty, and you are, moreover, represented to me as turbulent and defiant of the laws and institutions of your country."

*- Prophet John Taylor's account of the interview
between General Ford and President Smith,
Teachings of the Prophet Joseph Smith, p. 334*

"The legality of the action of the Mayor and City Council was, of course, questionable, though some sought to defend it on legal grounds; but it must be conceded that neither proof nor argument for legality are convincing."

- LDS Historian B.H. Roberts,
History of the Church,
Introduction to v.6, p. XXXVIII

"… there was no legal justification in 1844 for the destruction of the Expositor press as a nuisance."

- Utah Law Review,
Summer 1965, pp. 890-891.

"… when Joseph Smith ordered the actual destruction of the Nauvoo Expositor printing press he provided his enemies with a clearly legitimate means of arresting him for violation of the law. They seized upon this to inflame the public even more, and this led directly to the assassination. Some people may be disturbed by the suggestion that Joseph Smith acted illegally in this instance, but it is important to understand that under the tense pressure of the times he too, may have made a mistake."

- BYU Today,
March 1976, p. 10

"Joseph Smith, acting as mayor, ordered the city marshall [sic] to destroy the newspaper and press without delay and instructed the major general of the Nauvoo legion to have the militia assist. Shortly after eight o'clock that evening, citizens and legionnaires marched to the 'Expositor' office and smashed the press, scattering the type as they did so. This act infuriated the non-Mormons of Hancock County, who saw it as a final act of contempt for their laws. The 'Quincy Whig' denounced the 'high-handed outrage' and said that if this was a specimen of 'Mormon attitude toward

law and rights it is not surprising that the Missourians were raised to madness and drove them from the state.'.... To provide justification for a march on Nauvoo, charges of prompting a riot were made up against Smith and several Mormon leaders, and Constable David Bettisworth was sent to Nauvoo on June 12 to apprehend them.... Emissaries were sent to Governor Ford, charging that Smith had defied the law and asking Ford to bring the state militia.... In the face of an imminent attack on his city, Smith declared Nauvoo under martial law and called out the Legion, a defensive action which later led to treason charges levied against him at Carthage.... he [Governor Ford] wrote the Mormon leader requesting that evidence be shown to justify the actions taken against the 'Expositor.' After reviewing this and counter evidence from anti-Mormons, Ford wrote Smith on the next day, denouncing the city's proceedings as unlawful and demanding that those involved in the move against the 'Expositor' submit to the processes of the law at Carthage."

- Carthage Conspiracy,
by Oaks and Hill,
pp. 15-16

"The destruction of libelous 'prints and papers' can scarcely be held to sustain the action of destroying a 'printing press.'"

- LDS Historian B.H. Roberts,
History of the Church,
v. 7, p. 91, footnote